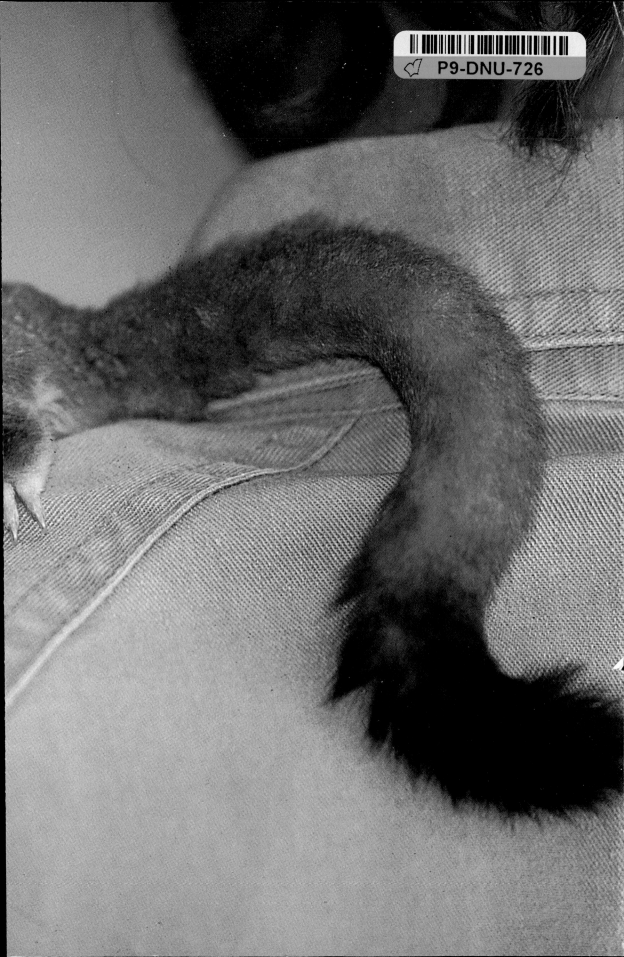

CONTENTS

t.f.h.

Distributed in the UNITED STATES to the Pet Trade by T.F.H. Publications, Inc., One T.F.H. Plaza, Neptune City, NJ 07753; distributed in the UNITED STATES to the Bookstore and Library Trade by National Book Network, Inc. 4720 Boston Way, Lanham MD 20706; in CANADA to the Pet Trade by H & L Pet Supplies Inc., 27 Kingston Crescent, Kitchener, Ontario N2B 2T6; Rolf C. Hagen Inc., 3225 Sartelon St. Laurent-Montreal Quebec H4R 1E8; in CANADA to the Book Trade by Vanwell Publishing Ltd., 1 Northrup Crescent, St. Catharines, Ontario L2M 6P5 ; in ENGLAND by T.F.H. Publications, PO Box 15, Waterlooville PO7 6BQ; in AUSTRALIA AND THE SOUTH PACIFIC by T.F.H. (Australia), Pty. Ltd., Box 149, Brookvale 2100 N.S.W., Australia; in NEW ZEALAND by Brooklands Aquarium Ltd. 5 McGiven Drive, New Plymouth, RD1 New Zealand; in Japan by T.F.H. Publications, Japan—Jiro Tsuda, 10-12-3 Ohjidai, Sakura, Chiba 285, Japan; in SOUTH AFRICA by Lopis (Pty) Ltd., P.O. Box 39127, Booysens, 2016, Johannesburg, South Africa. Published by T.F.H. Publications, Inc.

MANUFACTURED IN THE
UNITED STATES OF AMERICA
BY T.F.H. PUBLICATIONS, INC.

A New Owner's Guide to SUGAR GLIDERS

Helen O'Reilly

INTRODUCING Sugar Gliders

In recent years there has been a considerable upsurge of interest in all exotic animals, be they mammals, birds, reptiles or fish that fall within this category of pets. Of the mammals, the little sugar glider is second only to the hedgehog in popularity. Like that prickly ball of spines, it's unusual: it's the first representative from its scientific order to gain high popularity. If you are seeking a pet that is very different from the average pet—such as a rabbit, hamster, dog, or cat—this little cuddly critter just might be the answer. It has the virtues of being very cute, companionable, and easy to care for. It does not make a noise that will upset your neighbors, as might a parrot or dog, and you won't need to take it out for walks.

It will live very well in an apartment because its housing will not take up a lot of space. If obtained when young, you can expect your new friend to live an average of 10 years, with 14 not unheard of when raised in domestic conditions. This is a good lifespan for such a relatively small mammal.

The sugar glider is becoming a popular pet. It has a long, luxurious tail and is the first marsupial to become accepted world-wide as a house pet.

POTENTIAL PROBLEMS

No pet is without some drawbacks, and the sugar glider is no exception. Because it's an exotic pet it is subject to more federal and state regulations than animals regarded as domestic, such a dogs, rabbits, and guinea pigs. This fact alone means potential owners living in certain states, even areas within these, cannot legally keep these pets.

Unlike the hedgehog, the sugar glider is a very social animal that must either have the company of its own kind or an owner who has ample time to spend with the pet. If a sugar glider is left for long periods without company it will be a very sad animal.

Like all pets, the sugar glider has its own husbandry needs. If these are neglected it will prove to be less than the perfect pet, but this is true of all animals. It is not a pet that should be obtained for a child on an impulse. Children have the habit of quickly losing interest in animals once the novelty has worn thin. This will badly affect the pet if the children are expected to attend daily chores of cleaning and feeding their little friends.

Sugar gliders are relatively small as you can see by comparing it to a hand size.

As an adult, you must accept total responsibility for the day-to-day needs of the sugar glider, or not own one in the first place. Any pet must be a commitment for the entire life of that animal. Anything less, reflects lack of owner responsibility, and the world already has enough of such people.

You may wish to own one of these pets because you have been told many people are making big dollars breeding them and other exotics. Forget such advice—you are not being told the full story. This book will explain the hard reality for those thinking the sugar glider is an investment animal, rather than a companion.

In the following chapters you will find all the information needed to obtain and maintain a sugar glider in the peak of health. Because this exotic animal is still a relatively new pet you should give extra consideration to its total needs before buying one.

PROFILE Of the Sugar Glider

The term **sugar glider** is the most popular of the three common names applied to one of four species of small animals collectively known as **lesser gliding possums**. The other two names are the honey glider and, in its native homelands, the flying squirrel—but this term is totally incorrect because squirrels are rodents, sugar gliders are not. The scientific name for the sugar glider is *Petaurus breviceps*. Its Latin meaning (*Petaurus*) is acrobat—one that flies through the air—so it's very appropriate to this mammal. It is native to northeastern Australia, New Guinea, the Bismark Archipelago, and some islands within this geographical range.

The other species of lesser gliders are *P. norfolcensis*, the squirrel glider of Australia; *P. abidi*, the Papuan glider of New Guinea; and *P. australis*, the fluffy glider of Australia. These other species are not generally available outside of their native ranges. This is especially so of the Australian species because that country banned the export of its native flora and fauna in 1959.

The name *sugar glider* is a popular name with no scientific status. It has other names in other countries. It belongs to a group called *lesser gliding possums*.

It is essential for the sugar glider to have a nest box in which to hide.

MARSUPIALS - UNUSUAL MAMMALS

The sugar glider is an unusual mammal because, unlike all other pets you will be familiar with, it's the first marsupial to gain popularity as a domestic animal. Of the 4,500 mammals on earth just 280 of them are marsupials. These differ from other mammals in numerous ways, but it is their reproductive system that especially distinguishes them from other mammalian orders (scientific groups).

Whereas most mammals develop their embryos to an advanced offspring state within a placenta before finally giving birth to them, the marsupial's system is two-stage. First the embryo develops for a very short period in an incomplete placenta. It then travels down the median vaginal opening (birth canal) to the outside world. Here it crawls, unaided, towards the abdomen, where it takes hold on a nipple. This instantly starts to swell so the baby is firmly held in place.

In most marsupials, including the sugar glider, the female has an abdominal pouch in which the nipples are located. This has a small opening into which the babies crawl as they seek a nipple. As the babies grow, the pouch becomes a home for them until they are large enough to live independently. The order Marsupialia is named for this pouch (marsupium), even though some members do not have one. In such cases a small flap of skin extends around each nipple. The babies literally cling to their mother, as well as to her nipple, during their formative period.

Although some marsupials are

Sugar gliders reproduce differently than many familiar mammals. The embryo develops in an incomplete placenta when it leaves the body cavity to seek one of its mother's nipples to which it attaches.

The sugar glider is a marsupial because it has a marsupium, otherwise known as a belly pouch. Marsupials are found mainly in and around Australia.

distributed in North and South America, most species are native to New Guinea, Australia and islands in those regions. It is thought marsupials first appeared in North America, migrated to South America, then to Australia via Antarctica before that island continent separated from South America and Antarctica. With no major eutherian mammals to compete with (those with fully developed placentas) they were able to proliferate.

This is why Australia has so many diverse forms of marsupials. Examples are kangaroos, wallabies, the koala bear, wombats, marsupial mice, opossums, bandicoots, quolls (native marsupial cats), and other species. Some authorities regard the marsupials as primitive mammals that were unable to compete with the placental mammals, but this view is beginning to change.

There is clear evidence that certain species are able to successfully compete with eutherians when the two share the same ecological niche. This suggests there are some advantages in the marsupial reproductive strategy. This apart, selective marsupials have exhibited a capacity to learn that exceeds that of some of the eutherian mammals previously regarded as having superior intellect.

Taking all factors into account, the marsupials may have been unfairly regarded in past years. A better way of viewing them is they are not primitive inferior mammals, but a group that had less opportunity to spread with the passing years because their main center of distribution (Australia), being a large island, was a very important evolutionary limiting factor.

Marsupials, like sugar gliders, kangaroos, and opossums, etc.,are the lowest order of mammals. They bear imperfect young which are carried in a pouch. Inside the pouch are the mother's breast nipples which furnish nourishment while the young animal matures. Photo by Wil P. Mara.

Sugar gliders eat and act a lot like squirrels but they are not even closely related. Squirrels are rodents! Sugar gliders are known by their scientific name of *Petaurus breviceps*. Photo by Wil P. Mara.

SCIENTIFIC NAMES

You may have wondered why zoologists apply Latin-based names to animals, making life complicated for the average owner or hobbyist. The fact is, the system in place actually makes things easier internationally. Latin and Greek were the two classical languages used throughout the western world as it developed.

It is hardly surprising that to avoid language barriers scientists adopted a language that could be used in any current language as the sciences became a more and more important part of our lives. Latin, being a dead language, was the natural choice. Greek and other languages have since been integrated in the system of naming animals devised by the Swedish naturalist Carolus Linnaeus during the 18th century.

Common names can result in much confusion because they are not bound by any regulations—scientific names are. Further, the name sugar glider would mean nothing to a person who did not speak English—and the same was true for the name given to that animal in France, Germany or Russia. *Petaurus breviceps* is very specific, so it remains the same in every counrty.

Further, no other living organism can have this name, so it's unique to this particular life form. Many animals could have the same

A very healthy-looking sugar glider on top of the hollowed log which is her home. Photo by Wil P. Mara.

common names. The first part of the scientific name indicates the genus the animal is placed in. The second part of the name, called the trivial or specific name, indicates the individual group (species) of animal within that genera.

All animal species have two-part names to distinguish them from any other animal. The scientific name always appears in a text differing that of the main text, thus italics is the usual choice. The generic name always begins with a capital letter, the trivial name always with a lower case.

If regional or other variants of a species are given recognition (this often being a debatable status) they are called a subspecies and have a three-part name. The first

two names indicate the species, the third indicates the particular form of that species. The system is controlled internationally by many regulations. It has proved to be very successful in spite of some inherent problems.

A species is best described as a group of individuals that, allowing for sexual differences, look similar and will interbreed quite freely in their natural habitat. They will produce fertile offspring that resemble themselves of the appropriate sex. Although these scientific explanations may have little interest to some pet owners, the potential dedicated hobbyist or breeder should be familiar with them. They are obligatory knowledge when reading scientific texts.

SUGAR GLIDER DESCRIPTION

The sugar glider ranges in total length from 24-32cm (9.4-12in). Half of this comprises the furry tail. Average weight is about 135g (4.8 oz) for a male, somewhat less for a female. However, a well-fed female may be the same weight, or heavier, than a smaller male, or a male on a more restricted diet.

Each of the sugar glider's four feet has five toes. These are clawed except for the inner big toes (hallux) of the rear feet, which are adapted for climbing and grasping branches. Having no claws on their big toes reduces the risk that these could get caught on the branch at the moment the animal wishes to let go and glide from one tree or branch to another.

The basic color is a gray agouti ranging from dark to light with, in certain individuals, some suffusion of red-brown on the hindquarters that extends into the tail. A clear black median stripe extends from the nose to the root of the tail, after which it becomes indistinct. The underparts are very pale, usually a cream color, but with some yellow suffusion. This suffusion is not always caused by pigmentation. It can be the result of the fur being stained by urine, bedding, foods, and/or sweat gland secretion.

The gliding membrane is readily apparent as a fold of loose skin extending from the front to hind legs along the edge of the lower chest and abdomen. On the crown of males can be seen a grayish spot

Sugar gliders reach about one foot in length. Half of this length is the furry tail! They weigh under 5 ounces. They have five toes on each foot. Each toe has a claw except the inner big toes of the rear feet. Photo by Wil P. Mara.

that divides the stripe at that point—it is one of three glands used for scent marking. The other two are sternal and urogenital, the female having pouch and urogenital glands for this purpose.

The sexes are distinguished by the fact the male has a swelling (its scrotum) where the human navel is. This area is smooth in the female. The male's crown scent gland is another sexual feature. The pouch (marsupium) of a female will indicate her sex, though this only becomes apparent when she is ready to breed.

SOCIAL LIFE IN THE WILD

Sugar gliders are nocturnal animals, a fact indicated by their large, round eyes. They are arboreal, meaning they spend most of their time in tress, though they do descend to ground level in order to forage for some food items. They sleep in branch hollows that they line with leaves. They move from tree to tree by launching themselves into the air and spreading their gliding membrane.

They cannot fly, but have been known to glide for distances up to 45m (150 ft). The height from which they start, and prevailing winds, obviously affect how far they can travel. By adjusting the gliding membrane and the position of the tail, they have a high degree of directional control. As they reach their landing point they will arch their backs so the membrane acts as a brake, and so their legs are best positioned to grasp a branch.

These animals are omnivorous, meaning they eat foods of both animal and vegetable origin. Their diet includes insects, larvae, spiders, very small mammals, tree

Sugar gliders are nocturnal, meaning they become active at night. That's why they have such big eyes—to let more night light in.

Sugar gliders can jump ("glide") some distance (up to 150 feet), usually landing on your curtains at home. If you are fussy about such things, get a large cage in which you can confine your sugar glider, or don't get a sugar glider as a pet. NEVER confine a sugar glider to a small hamster cage. Photo by Wil P. Mara.

Sugar gliders are very social animals. If you only have one of them it might very well adopt YOU as its mother, brother or sister. This can create a special bond if you spend a lot of time with your sugar glider. Photo by Wil P. Mara.

sap, blossoms, fruit and vegetables. They are also very partial to nectar, which is reflected in their name: sugar, or honey glider.

Sugar glideres are very social animals. They live in small family units of up to seven adults, plus their young offspring of up to two years old. The adults will include at least one or two mature males. These will defend the family's immediate territory against other glider families, as well as help rear the youngsters.

Communication is by scent and vocalizations. The scent of each family is unique to it. It is spread to each member during social interactions, as well as specifically by the dominant male of a group. Vocalizations range from high-pitched sounds when the glider is angry to a chattering noise that's a sort of alarm call. More muted sounds are used during general communication between the family members.

Sugar gliders have many natural enemies, including birds of prey, snakes, large lizards, foxes, native cats, and domestic dogs and cats. They are also negatively affected by deforestation, though their population numbers are presently considered safe. They were introduced to Tasmania during the 19th century and are now well establish on that island.

Although a new pet in the United States, sugar gliders have been kept for many years in zoos where they have proved to be excellent subjects and readily bred. They have been maintained in many private collections, and were for a period popular pets in their homelands.

The hollowed log is the sugar glider's home and he will defend it against invasion by other gliders. Photo by Wil P. Mara.

HOUSING Your Sugar Glider

I t is very important that you obtain your sugar glider's housing before you obtain your sugar glider. This has a number of advantages. It allows you as much time as needed to find exactly the right size and style of cage to meet your personal preferences *and* the needs of the new pet. It avoids the risk you might rush the cage purchase because you are also obtaining the pet on the same day. This is never a sound way to proceed.

By visiting many pet stores you may discover the cage you really like is more costly than you had thought. Not having to purchase at that moment enables you the opportunity to delay acquiring the sugar glider while you save the extra cash. Always obtain the very best accommodation possible—it will prove to be a better long-term investment, and a better home for the sugar glider.

The proper cage will have room to accomodate the sugar glider and accessories such as a hollowed log. Photo by Wil P. Mara.

When you do obtain the housing, together with the necessary furnishings, you can set it all up so it is ready for immediate occupancy. You can also try it in a number of locations to satisfy yourself that it will meet your practical needs and those of the pet, which will be discussed shortly. Once the home is ready you can devote your energies to seeking the perfect sugar glider(s) for it.

ACCOMMODATION GUIDELINES

Any form of animal accommodation must meet certain basic criteria common to all housings. Beyond these, it must take account of the animal species, its size, and any special requirements that will make its life more comfortable.

Basic Needs: The housing should be well constructed so it's safe from two viewpoints. One is there must be no sharp projections on which your pet could get hurt, the other is it must be such that the pet cannot escape from it. It must also be constructed of materials that will enable you to clean it without problems. It must have a door large enough for you to get your arm in to reach all areas of the cage.

Species Needs: The sugar glider

This is the way a sugar glider sleeps inside a hollow log.

is arboreal, so the cage must have as much height as possible. This enables the pet to climb upwards where it will feel safe. If this is not possible there is an increased risk it will suffer from stress. This will slow down its immune system, making it more susceptible to health problems than would be the case with a non-stressed pet.

Although the sugar glider is not a large animal, the more space it has to live in the better. This enables you to furnish the housing so it's esthetically pleasing, yet gives the pet plenty of room in which to exercise and occupy itself when you are not at home. A small cage is a very sad home for any animal.

SIZE AND CONSTRUCTION MATERIALS

Taking account of the factors discussed, the minimum sized cage should have a base area of about 38 x 38 cm (15 x 15 in) and a height of 92 cm (36 in). But do remember, if you can supply a home much larger than this it will be far better. The size stated would be adequate for one or a pair, but for more than this you will need a larger size.

The preferred cage materials will

be all wire over a plastic or light metal (usually aluminum) base. The ideal wire hole size should be 2.5 x 1.25 cm (1 x $^1/_2$ in), but one inch square will be suitable for adults, less so for very small babies. The actual wire may be galvanized, epoxy, or chromium. Galvanized is by far the most popular, but it does come in various grades of finish. Try to obtain a cage featuring smooth weld points and a nice polished sheen to it. This will be easier to keep clean.

DESIGN FEATURES

Unlike the situation for well-established pets, there are not at this time any cages manufactured specifically for the sugar glider. However, this is not important because the ideal features of such cages are available in the form of those for birds. The ideal home will be an indoor aviary. These are produced in a range of sizes from modest to very large. Those large enough to be free standing on the floor (often on small wheels) are as good as you could get for these pets. They make

Study the components of this cage carefully as it has proven very successful for housing sugar gliders. Unfortunately there is no such thing (now) as a commercial sugar glider cage, but a sturdy indoor bird aviary has been used successfully.

perfect habit houses, as well as great cages for sugar glider families.

Somewhat smaller, though almost as costly, are the many large finch cages. The advantage of a finch cage is the bars are closely spaced, thus secure. The bars of a parrot cage might be too far apart, depending on the design. Unsuitable homes for these pets would be any form of aquarium, small mammal cages, and small standard-sized bird cages.

From a practical viewpoint the following are features to consider. Some cages have detachable bases, which make cleaning easier. Others may have a sliding tray, or a metal grill over a sliding tray, so fecal matter and uneaten foods fall through to the base. You can purchase aprons to fit round the outside of the cage so that any debris falls into this and is channeled back into the base of the cage. This keeps the immediate area of the cage clean.

If you can't find a hollow log, you can try some large plastic piping and cut off a suitable length (about 12 inches). Be sure the pipe is sanitized.

You can have a cage in which one side, or a large part of it, opens to create a platform. This makes cleaning very easy and enables the pet to enter and leave its cage when it wants, assuming you are present to supervise its freedom. You can also have units in which the top opens to form a platform.

If you dislike weld wire floors an alternative to achieve the same objective is one covered with plastic slats. These are more gentle on a pet's feet, yet allow debris to fall to the floor, making them very hygienic. There is a very extensive range of options for you to choose from if you take the time to visit a number of pet stores. If none have exactly what you want they may be able to show you other designs they can special order.

CAGE FURNISHINGS

You will require the following furnishings for your pet's home.

Food and water containers: At least two pots will be required for food—one for soft foods of high moisture content, and one for dry foods. Water can be supplied via a gravity-fed water bottle or an open water pot. Bottles have the advantage of keeping the water clear of fecal matter and other debris. Open pots have the advantage of enabling the pet to drink in a more natural manner, but they may quickly become fouled unless placed where this is unlikely to happen—such as high up in the cage.

Both food and water pots must be situated with care. They should not be placed below branches or perches where they could be fouled

It is cruel to keep a sugar glider confined to a small bird cage or hamster cage where it can't get enough exercise.

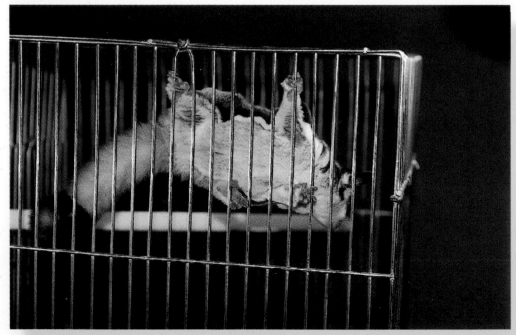

Food containers must have two compartments; one for soft, moist foods and the other for hard, dry foods.

with fecal droppings or urine. They can be placed onto feeding stations either hanging or fitted to the cage bars, or on the cage floor. If you have a family of sugar gliders it is wise to include two feeding areas to ensure each member gets their share of the food, and always has access to water.

Floor covering: You can cover this with natural wood fiber, granulated paper, or plain paper, though this tends to look less pleasing. Each of these has excellent absorbency and is biodegradable. Corn cob is another potential covering, but is harder on the feet and not especially absorbent. Do not use cedar shavings as the phenols in them can adversely affect the respiratory system, heart, and lungs.

The same is true, to a lesser extent, with white pine, though its low cost makes it a currently popular choice. Sawdust should be avoided because it can cling to moist foods, as well as being abrasive to the sexual organs and the pouch of breeding females.

Sand and clay or silicon cat litters are other coverings not recommended for these pets because of their abrasiveness and/or health dangers.

Branches & perches: Sugar gliders are natural climbers, so they need to have branches and/or perches in their cage. Branches should be those from fruit trees or other safe deciduous trees, such as willow, oak, and poplar. The leaves can be left on, but will soon fall off. Your pet will nibble on the bark, so

Massive feeding dishes are not required for sugar gliders because they must have fresh food every day. Don't allow the food to become stale.

the branches will need to be replaced once they become unsightly. A few stout branches can be retained on a permanent basis as long as they are regularly cleaned.

You can also feature commercial bird perches from your pet store. The best are those that have a

themselves from one end to the other.

Nestbox: The housing must feature a nestbox for the pet to sleep in. Without this it will become stressed. It should be located high in the cage, be securely fitted, yet easily removed for cleaning. The nestbox should be about 15 x 15 x

Food and water containers should be carefully located. They should not be found where droppings can contaminate them. Don't place them under perches of any kind.

variable diameter along their length. These provide good exercise for the glider's feet.

Arrange the perches in a climbing matrix, but be sure they are not located directly over open food or water pots. In a very large cage arrange perches so there's an open space with branches on either side of this. The gliders can then launch

15 cm (6 x 6 x 6 in) for a single pet, proportionately larger for two or more.

It should contain an excess hole large enough for the pet to enter without difficulty, but need not be an enormous hole. A nestbox designed for birds will work fine; plastic is an excellent choice because it is easy to keep clean.

If food is offered in a large open container, like a dish, be sure to empty and wash it every day. It must be thoroughly washed to sterilize it.

If the nestbox is wooden choose one that is screwed together, rather than nailed, or one with a removable or hinged top or side. These can be more readily sanitized. You can also paint their internal surfaces with a non-lead based paint. Gliders will urinate in their nestbox, so the more easily it can be cleaned the less odor it will generate. Cover the floor of this with as their location. This will be appreciated and encourage breeding willingness.

Exercise wheel: The items discussed are obligatory in any cage regardless of its size. If space permits you might include a large exercise wheel. However, it must be of the solid tread type. There must be no risk at all that the glider's tail could in any way get caught as the

A hamster exercise wheel is perfect for the sugar glider and ensures it will get enough exercise.

your chosen floor covering. Do not use hay because this may be harboring fungal spores or parasitic eggs that will hatch in the damp, warm, environment of the nestbox.

If you have a family of gliders you can place two nestboxes in the cage, which will be useful if you attempt to breed your pets. It gives them a choice of nestboxes, as well wheel revolves. This means those that revolve between a framework are unsuitable. The access must be totally open.

Toys: A swing or ball on stout string suspended from the roof of the cage will no doubt become an amusing plaything for your pet.

The same is true of ladders that lead to a food or tidbit shelf.

Anything they can climb up, or between, will help occupy their minds. Be sure nothing supplied has sharp edges or projections that could be dangerous, or is made of flimsy plastic or a similar material that would be dangerous if chewed and swallowed.

TEMPERATURE & HUMIDITY

Sugar gliders will live comfortably within the temperature range of 70-80°F (21-27°C). This is about the same as your own comfort range. It is always best if the temperature stays reasonably constant, though a few degrees of movement over a 24-hour period will not adversely affect them. This would happen in the wild. Relative humidity is best in the range of 50-65 percent. Avoid very dry air because these animals evolved to live in regions normally quite moist.

Temperatures above the optimum stated will increase the risk of heat stress. This should be remembered when transporting—more important, leaving—a glider in a car on a hot summer day. Be sure there is ample ventilation. Although gliders are from tropical countries, bear in mind they are nocturnal. This means they are active during the cooler parts of the 24-hour cycle, and are not subjected to direct, intense sunlight. Very dangerous to any pet, especially ones from tropical climates and those housed in cages, is sudden changes in temperature and humidity. These induce chills and generally lower resistance to illness. Breeders, especially, should always ensure there is ample fresh air within breeding rooms. The lack of

Sugar gliders love to sleep and rest in a dark cave. A small bird house suits them perfectly but be sure that the bird house can be cleaned, as sugar gliders urinate in their sleeping quarters.

The bottom of the cage should have ample covering which is urine absorbent. Ask your pet shop personnel what they suggest for flooring. Do NOT use cedar or white pine chips. Photo by Wil P. Mara.

this is a major factor in the spread of disease.

By keeping the air moving you reduce the risk that pathogenic (disease-causing) organisms will remain—they will be removed from the breeding or stock room via the air current created by the ventilation system. If humidity is suddenly allowed to fall below normal levels the result will be that any pathogens held within water droplets will be released into the air.

LOCATING THE CAGE

Given the foregoing comments, the following situations should be avoided:

1. Never locate the cage where it will be subject to direct sunlight from which the glider cannot escape, and which will result in sudden temperature fluctuations. The obvious example would be in front of a window.

2. Never locate the cage facing exterior doors, or those which connect two rooms that may be of different heat levels. These will create drafts that will rapidly change the cage temperature.

3. Never locate the cage above or adjacent to any heating or cooling units. These will rapidly change the cage temperature as they switch on and off.

It is also preferable that when your pet is sitting on a favored branch or perch this should be approximately at your head height.

Avoid locating the cage such that you would always be above the height of the sugar glider. This will intimidate it, tending to increase its stress. Always try to consider the pet's natural desire to be above what's going on around it. This will help ensure it feels secure. A mentally relaxed animal always makes a better pet.

CHOOSING A Sugar Glider

With the housing purchased and in place you can now turn your thoughts to purchasing one or more sugar gliders. Never rush this, otherwise you may quickly have reason to regret it. You should determine your priorities before you go shopping—and stick to them. We will discuss all major considerations—legal status in your state, source, health, age, choice of sex, and temperament.

Purchasing your sugar glider requires a lot of thought as to legality (is it permitted in your town?), danger to the pet, and your ability to tender to the sugar glider's needs.

Is It Legal?

All animals are subject to local, state, and federal regulations. Popular pet species, such as dogs, cats, rabbits, birds and fish, have fewer restrictions than those regarded as exotic or "wild." The sugar glider is an exotic pet also classified as wildlife by some authorities. This means you must check with your state wildlife department or the USDA (United States Dept. of Agriculture) whether it can legally be kept in your state. Do not accept the advice of any other source. Even people who ordinarily would give you good advice—such as breeders and pet store owners—could be misinformed; it happens.

When any "new" pet arrives, the agencies mentioned have a number of factors to consider before they decide whether it (mammal, reptile, bird, fish or invertebrate) should be allowed as a pet. These factors are as follows:

1. Is it dangerous?

2. Could it represent a major health risk to its owner and the public at large?

3. If it escaped, could it survive and establish its species in the wild?

4. If it did, what effect would this have on indigenous species of flora and fauna?

5. Is it classified as endangered in its country of origin?

6. Is the average pet owner capable of catering to its needs with no risk they will cause it to suffer because its husbandry might require special knowledge?

By examining the stomach of the sugar glider you can ascertain its sex as the male has diagnostic bulges around its navel.

The need for these considerations, and the resulting legislation, is historical. The fact is, indigenous species have been transported from their country of origin and have had a devastating effect in other countries. Dangerous pets have been kept by people not qualified to keep them, and pet owners have abandoned exotic pets in the wild. Their irresponsible acts have prompted agencies to react accordingly.

The reality of this situation is that you may legally keep a sugar glider in some states, not in others. Never keep these pets if your state forbids it, even if you know of people who are doing so. They are doing what has just been discussed—acting irresponsibly. They can be heavily fined. They merely provide more ammunition for those who campaign that all exotic pets should be banned, and that more legislation should be enacted for pets currently classified as "domestic."

Even if your state allows these pets you must check there are no local ordinances that forbid them. Both state and local legislation can be reversed if enough knowledgeable people can present a sound case for so doing. This is more likely to be successful at the local than state level. But you cannot try to reverse local regulations forbidding them if the state forbids the pet— they are the higher authority.

WHERE TO PURCHASE?

There are only two sources you should consider. Pet shops and breeders. For the vast majority of owners the pet shop is the logical choice, and usually the most convenient. Apart from the pet itself they will be able to supply all your present and future equipment needs, and are there on a day-to-day basis to answer your queries.

It is important the supplier meets certain standards of both care and knowledge. The pets should be housed in spacious cages that are obviously cleaned on a regular basis. Water should always be present. The general cleanliness of

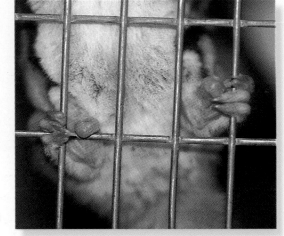

The sugar glider has five toes on each foot, but only the rear inside thumbs are missing claws.

the store itself should satisfy you its owners are very professional in their management.

The seller should be able to tell you the age and sex of the glider, as well as be informed on its correct management. They should be able to answer most of the questions you are likely to ask, including those related to your own situation and if the glider is likely to prove the right pet for you. Be wary of those who are clearly only interested in selling you a pet, rather than if it is suited to your situation. Hopefully, you have purchased this book before obtaining the glider. You will already know the right answers to your questions— but ask them anyway.

You are strongly advised to purchase only a domestically bred pet, not one that was caught in the wild. There is no shortage of domestic gliders. They make infinitely better pets. You will know their age, and be assured that they are less stressed than wild-caught individuals. There is little justification in encouraging the trade in wild-caught animals once a good domestic stock level is established, which it has been with the sugar glider.

Before you buy a sugar glider be sure it looks healthy, active and alert. It should also be tame.

THE HEALTHY SUGAR GLIDER

Above any other criteria, a pet must be healthy when you obtain it. If you are in any way unsure of this, *do not* purchase the glider—it could prove a costly mistake. Ask the seller what guarantee of health they offer, if any, with their pets, and ask if this is in writing. Do not allow a guarantee to cloud your judgment of good health; the pet's immediate health should be the only basis for obtaining it.

A seller can supply you with a signed health certificate from their veterinarian, but you will be charged extra for this. Because good health can so quickly turn to illness it really is very important you have total trust in the seller.

If you are able to observe the gliders moving around this is ideal.

They may retreat to their nestbox as you approach the cage, however, those that have been well socialized to humans by their breeder will not do this—a good starting sign. You do not want one that shows any difficulty in its movements. If one appears disinterested in what is going on around it when others are on the move this is a bad sign. It may be feeling unwell. The problem may only be minor but you cannot, at that time, be sure of this.

Satisfied as to the general activity level, select a sugar glider that seems outgoing and unafraid of your close proximity to the cage. The store assistant will take the animal out so you can more carefully examine it, maybe even hold it.

Good health is not really difficult

The seller of your sugar glider should be able to supply you with a health certificate from a veterinarian. It costs more but is worth it. Photo by Wil P. Mara.

The coat of the sugar glider should be thick and dry; no ulcers or bald spots should be observed. Photo by Wil P. Mara.

to assess. The following are all signs of potential problems. None of them should be visible in the glider you're considering. If one is, be cautious in accepting any reason the seller gives.

The eyes should be large, round and bold, never sunken, cloudy or weeping. The nose will be just slightly moist, never obviously wet and discharging any liquid. The ears are erect and should display no sores, wax-like encrustations, or signs of parasites. The anal region should be clean, not stained or caked with congealed fecal matter in the fur. There are five toes on each foot and each toe has a claw except the inner ones of the hind feet.

A missing toe, or one with no claw (injuries happen) is not a major problem to the animal, but is not desirable, especially in a prospective breeding glider. The missing part may be of a genetic cause, not from an injury.

Carefully brush the fur backward to see if any parasites are observed—or signs of their activity. This will be in the form of clusters of dark specks (their fecal matter or eggs), or evidenced by white specks/powder at the base of the hair shafts. This is caused by mites that bury into the hairs or skin. There should be no bald areas of fur, sores, lumps or other swellings.

Be sure to hold the pet so its gliding membrane can be inspected for any signs of parasites or problems. The fur covers the entire body and tail and should be dense all over, displaying obvious "spring" and condition, never dry and lifeless.

Although you cannot inspect the teeth in any detail, you should ascertain that they look healthy and that the jaws are not misaligned. This means one should not protrude beyond the other,

weeks. Moving into a new environment is very stressful for even a well socialized pet. The fewer the changes it has to contend with the better.

WHAT AGE?

Sugar gliders become independent of their mother when they're about four months old. Females are physically mature when they're about nine months,

When you buy a new sugar glider, be sure to ascertain its feeding regimen. Stay on this diet for a week or so until the glider becomes accustomed to its new surroundings. Photo by Wil P. Mara.

leaving a gap. This condition is called malocclusion and can make feeding difficult. It is one of the genetic problems that can arise with poorly bred domestic stock.

When you have selected your new pet be sure you receive a copy of its current feeding regimen. This should be maintained for the first week while the pet settles into its new home. If any changes in the diet are needed these should be done gradually in the subsequent

males about one year, though in both instances they may reach sexual maturity earlier than this. Never purchase a youngster that is not fully independent of its mother. This will dramatically increase the risk of problems.

If you are obtaining breeding stock the following is probably the preferred order for the novice breeder.

1. Proven young breeding pair or trio. These will be the most costly, but should ensure offspring and that the parents will care for these as they should.

2. Young, proven adult and unproven individual. Ideally, the female should be the experienced one.

3. Youngsters never previously bred, but now at breeding age. You can at least be satisfied they have matured into nice sugar gliders displaying no problems.

This is an important consideration for a novice.

CHOICE OF SEX?

If you want a pet glider, its sex is not a major factor. Other aspects, such as health, age, and how tame it is are more important. All these things being equal, a female will be the preferred choice for most owners. This is because the male uses his scent glands to mark

Buying youngsters not previously bred usually is the best way to get started. But they are not necessarily the best pets if you intend to raise a sugar glider family. Photo by Wil P. Mara.

4. Weaned youngsters not yet physically mature. This is the least costly option. You must not only wait for the gliders to mature, but hope they prove totally compatible and of good conformation. However, there is an advantage in having to wait some months. You gain practical experience, and the gliders will be familiar with their home.

territory more than the female does.

However, if you are attending regular cleaning chores as you should, this should not affect your choice because the scent is not especially strong.

The other advantage of a female is that if you decide to have two gliders these will live together without the problem of unwanted

In terms of being a pet, either a male or female is acceptable. It is more important to get a young, healthy and tame animal.

babies, which is sure to happen if you keep one of each sex together. Two males will also live amicably if they are reared together from youngsters—as long as you never subsequently introduce a female, which will result in fighting between the males.

TEMPERAMENT

Your entire future enjoyment of a sugar glider is going to revolve around its temperament. This being so, you should give your glider's temperament major consideration. This is as important as good health. Indeed, if the pet's temperament is not of the required level, there is every chance its health may suffer later on. This is because when a pet does not meet owner expectations it tends to be the forgotten member of the family. Consequently, day-to-day chores are not attended as they

should be, and physical examination of the pet (being difficult) is postponed to a later date that never seems to be come. When problems arrive, they go unnoticed. Matters go downhill from there.

Although temperament has a genetic base it is also heavily influenced by the environment the pet is reared in. What happens during the first three months of its life—before you obtain it—will shape its future potential to make the perfect pet. If the breeder does not interact with his stock, and handle the babies, they will not be imprinted on humans. No amount of subsequent affectionate handling will ever make them as good as they could have been.

Every level of temperament in a youngster is sold, from those that are little short of screeching monsters to those that are truly

Aside from its health, nothing is more important than a sugar glider's temperament and friendliness (tameness).

If you can't hold your sugar glider like this, which is comfortable both for the owner and the animal, then a proper relationship doesn't exist.

adorable. You want the latter. Be sure you get it. When you are selecting a pet, watch how it reacts to the seller when it is removed from its cage. If the pet quickly seeks a place of retreat this tells you it was never fully socialized by its breeder. It should not display overt fear.

The ideal pet will be easy to take from its cage. It will happily sit on the seller's hand, arm, or shoulder, allowing itself to be stroked. It may be apprehensive when you hold it, but should not panic. It will settle down after a minute or so.

When being handled it should not be struggling to get away, nor be squealing and defecating, which would indicate it received little previous handling. If it's a youngster you will, by regular gentle handling, be able to make it much tamer, but it may never be the affectionate pet you really

wanted. The more mature the individual, the more important this advice is. There will have been a longer time for the pet's behavior patterns to become part of its general nature, thus much harder to change.

With breeding stock it can be argued that temperament is not as important. The down side is babies will quickly learn to react by mimicking their parents. If these are nervous, the babies will pick up on this and take longer to imprint than those with very placid parents.

The final advice is that if you do not find exactly the right sugar glider the first time you visit your local pet stores, do not purchase one. Instead, tell your preferred store what you want. They will either be able to obtain it, or tell you when they may be expecting further stock from a different source.

SUGAR GLIDERS As Pets

N o pet is perfectly suited to every potential owner. This reality should be given a lot of thought before you obtain any animal. It will save you becoming disenchanted, and the pet from living in a home where it is neither fully appreciated nor happy. Like all pets it offers certain advantages and certain drawbacks when compared with other pets you might choose. Your decision to have one in your home should be based entirely on its drawbacks. If these will not be a problem its virtues can then be considered. You will have reached a decision in the most logical manner.

Are you suitable to own a sugar glider? The pet will be 100% dependent upon you for its food, shelter and health. Be sure you are willing to fulfill your obligations before you acquire a sugar glider.

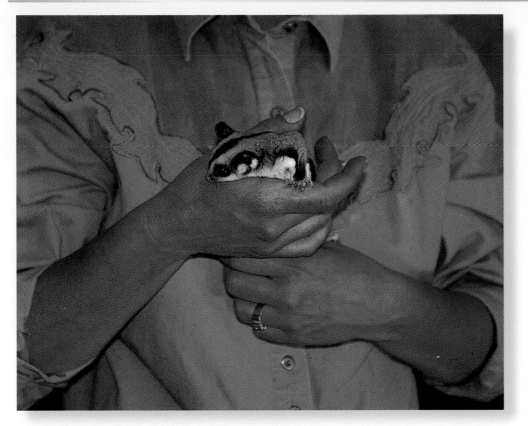

Sugar gliders are very delicate little pets and they must not be mishandled. Holding them loosely high above the ground could result in a dangerous fall.

THE PROBLEMS

Sugar gliders are delicate little mammals that are unsuited to homes where they may be roughly handled by small children.

To be fully companionable, almost any pet should be given as much time out of its housing as possible. This is true of the sugar glider, and it is the only way you can truly interact with it and make it a real friend. If you do not have the time to do this on a regular basis you will not make the ideal owner.

If you have other pets, such as dogs, cats, or ferrets running loose in your home, this is also a negative situation. It greatly increases the chances the glider will be injured or killed by one of these when it is out of its cage and you are not present to supervise matters. Even if you are, the pet could be injured faster than you could react to the situation.

Some pet owners are very house proud and should carefully reflect on the fact that these pets will climb up curtains and glide from one point of the room to another. They may defecate on the curtains or other objects they alight on. They may knock ornaments from shelves as they land on them, or as they inspect these out of curiosity.

If you do not clean the cage on a very regular basis it will start to smell. There are ways you can control odors these days, but the bottom line still requires regular cleaning. This means a complete strip-down of the cage every week, and daily cleaning to keep things tidy and remove excess fecal matter and uneaten foods.

You must also be a mindful person. This means you must not leave windows or doors open when should have a canopy to eliminate the risk the glider might accidentally land in the water.

The kitchen is an especially dangerous place for any "flying" pet, and especially for a sugar glider, which does not have a bird's ability to change direction and lift off if it approaches a hot surface. All of these situations mean the glider owner must be the sort who

It's fun to handle a sugar glider, but be sure you do it inside a safe room, with no open windows or doors and no access for a pet cat or dog.

your pet is out of its cage. You must always be thinking about the pet's safety. Open fires and extractor fans must have safety guards around them. Potential poisonous plants and electrical wiring should not be left where the glider might nibble on them. Cupboards containing poisonous chemicals must always be firmly closed. If you have an aquarium it is constantly aware where his pet is at every moment.

The ideal owners will be a family where any children are old enough to exercise responsible attitudes to caring and handling of these pets. The adults will obviously be house-proud, but willing to accept their little friend may get into mischief. They will also have to clean up after it. If it is to be banished to its

A good pet sugar glider likes to be handled and will develop a strong bond with its handler. In return, its owner must be able to accept the responsibility to clean up after it.

cage because it messes now and then when it is free, it is not suited to that sort of owner.

THE VIRTUES

Being a small, quiet, and inoffensive mammal, the sugar glider will make the perfect pet for the person living alone, for couples with no children, and for the families like those just discussed. The sugar glider has a really cute personality that is gentle, yet curious enough to get into mischief as it searches everything for tidbits.

Your sugar glider will happily sit on your hand, arm or shoulder, delighting in receiving your affection and little treats of food. You can even transport it around your home in your shirt pocket!

After all it spent all of its formative years in a similar place—its mother's pouch. It will regard this as a place where it feels secure.

If you have an enclosed patio containing vegetation or perches you can while away many hours watching your pet clamber up and down and gliding from one place to another.

THE GREAT OUTDOORS

It is very important that children are told their sugar glider must not be taken outdoors. If it is, it might be startled, whereupon it will head for the nearest tree. Once in the upper branches, it may decide to glide to other trees, and could soon be lost. It might also glide from buildings. When outdoors it is vulnerable to attack by dogs, cats

The sugar glider is the perfect pet for the person living alone or couple without children. It is a gentle, slightly mischievous animal that is constantly searching for food...or sleeping.

The height of tameness is when the sugar glider takes his food from your hand.

and other terrestrial critters. Once in trees it might be attacked by any large bird.

The only safe place for a sugar glider, when out of your home, would be in an unoccupied aviary with small-hole weld wire mesh.

During the warmer months this would make a fine place for a pair or more of these pets to enjoy some fresh air. The requirements of such an aviary are the same as those for birds—branches, perches, and a nestbox well protected from direct sunlight and inclement weather.

Controlling Odors

All pets release a particular body odor as well as the smell associated with their fecal matter. It is fecal matter that creates the most unwanted odors. They are a by-product of digestion in the form of ammonia gas and compounds. Additional to these are smells created by bacteria that cause the breakdown of any organic matter—especially that which is damp, such as uneaten fruits, vegetables and other fresh foods. These quickly begin to rot.

Cleaning encompasses the cage bars, floor, food and water pots, perches and nestbox. The floor covering material must be changed regularly so fecal matter and urine are not left to create additional odors by their action on the floor material, and on uneaten foods. The area around the cage must be cleaned daily because molecules of odor travel from the cage to this area and settle on carpets, chairs, and other porous surfaces.

Once a week the cage should be completely stripped and cleaned using a dilute solution of household bleach. Be sure to rinse this afterwards to remove all traces of the bleach, then allow to dry. You can purchase odor removers from your pet store. The ones to buy are those that contain enzymes that convert ammonium compounds into other compounds that are odorless.

Scented air fresheners, even some disinfectants, merely mask to control ammonia and its compounds in aquariums.

Another aid to odor control is an ionizer. Available in a range of sizes, they must be left on continually, but are economical to operate. They work by releasing millions of negative ions which attract airborne dust, bacteria and odor molecules, making them heavier than air. The molecules fall to the nearest surface and are removed by your regular cleaning. They are available from good pet

Sugar gliders can make an awful odor if they and their cages are not cleaned after they urinate or defecate. Some room deodorizers can help.

odors for a short period, they do not address the cause of the odor.

If you place an open pot of crushed aquarium charcoal near the cage this will help control odors because it absorbs the odor molecules. The same is true of zeolite. Charcoal cannot be "recharged"—once it reaches its capacity to adsorb it ceases to function. Zeolite can be soaked in a saline solution and will release its contents, thus being reusable. Both of these compounds are well known to aquarists who use them

shops or avicultural suppliers. Odor control aids do not negate the importance of regular cleaning, they simply help limit odors between such cleanings.

Sugar gliders are very easy to live with, making few demands on their owners. The key to success is to handle them frequently so they really do become members of the family, not just living objects in a cage. Give them the considerations discussed in this chapter and you will be delighted with them as newly acquired companions.

FEEDING Sugar Gliders

The sugar glider, based on feeding type, is an omnivore. This means it eats a diet that includes foods of both animal and plant origins. The ratio of one to the other is about 25% animal protein and 75% plant matter—fruits, vegetables, grain and their by-products. The complete dietary requirements of sugar gliders is not fully understood from a scientific viewpoint, a fact that's true for most animals. That which follows is based on the practical experiences of breeders and zoological institutions that have found it adequate to maintain good health and breeding capacity.

Sugar gliders are omnivores, which means they eat everything. Whether plant or animal, the sugar glider searches food out on a constant constant basis.

Domestic diet items can never duplicate those the animal would eat in the wild state, it being a case of supplying comparable foods that are likely to contain the same ingredients. One of the errors made by many pet owners (and breeders) is they reduce the diet to a few items so the feeding regimen is simple, low cost, and can be attended quickly. This policy is not conducive to ensuring the pet is receiving a balanced diet that contains all the proteins, fats, carbohydrates and vitamins needed to maintain peak health.

We must distinguish between a diet that is sufficient for the animal to survive on, and that which will increase the likelihood of the pet having maximum immunity from diseases, attainment of potential longevity, and no risk of stress syndromes caused by nutritional deficiencies.

Generally, non-professional pet breeders, and many pet shops, tend to feed Spartan diets. Many pet owners feed an excess of foods containing ingredients that will result in obesity—a major problem these days in many pet species. Feeding is therefore very much an acquired skill based on some knowledge of the major ingredients of given items, combined with the ability to assess peak condition in each individual.

If you feed soft, moist foods (like bananas) along with cereal (like sunflower seeds), the soft food will ruin the dry food in a matter of hours, so either feed in separate dishes or remove the food an hour or so after you offer it.

Even though sugar gliders will eat dry dog foods, it is not enough for their dietary balance. They need fresh fruits, flowers, seeds and living insects.

FEEDING CONSIDERATIONS

Before discussing food items there are a number of related topics that should always be kept in mind. They will influence what you feed, how much of it you should supply, and when. If overlooked, or not appreciated, dietary related problems are likely to follow.

Dietary Changes: One of the most common problems created by many pet owners is a sudden change in their pet's diet. This will come in two ways. They will read, or be told, that given items are good for their pets, so they provide a sudden glut of these. The second way is when they initially obtain the pet they will change the diet, often increasing the range because they feel the previous diet was Spartan. In both instances

digestive upsets are likely. These may lead the owner to believe the advice given was incorrect, or the pet has become ill for some other reason—the dietary method not being suspected.

The digestive process is very complicated. The system contains many bacteria that help break down foods into simple ingredients that are rebuilt into specific tissues (muscle, organs, blood and so on). Foods contain ingredients in different ratios to those same ingredients in other foods.

The digestive system functions based on what it's developed to cope with. If you suddenly make dietary changes the system speeds up, or slows down, dependent on the dietary ingredients.

The bacteria needed to break down given ingredients may not be

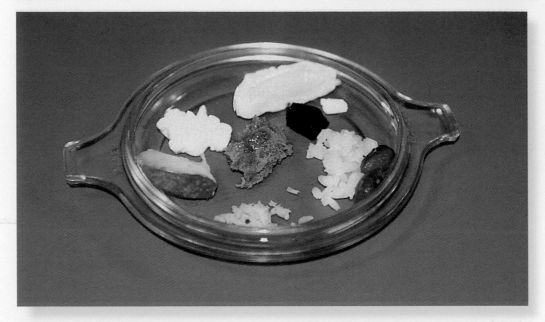

Being omnivores, sugar gliders need a variety of animal-and-vegetable-based foods. Low-fat meats with fresh fruits and some starches are all good for your pet.

able to cope with a sudden excess of these. The result is a temporary reduction in the efficiency of the system. Diarrhea (usually), or constipation, is the result. This tends to lower the efficiency of the immune system and secondary conditions may develop that can be more sinister than the initial minor tummy upset.

Dietary changes must always be gradual. Your sugar glider is well able to cope with a very extensive range of food items, but not if they are suddenly introduced together, or in a glut as individual items. This is why it is important for you to know what the seller was feeding your pet, and that you maintain this diet for at least a week before you introduce new items in small quantities. This is especially true when the pet's former diet was largely of a dry food type and you plan to increase the moist food content.

Food Preferences: Your sugar glider, like you, will display preferences and dislikes to certain foods. Some items will be relished by all gliders, others will be taken according to the individual's palate. Bear in mind also that because an item is initially refused does not mean it will be continually refused.

It may be a case that the pet has never tasted the item before, and it may need time to gradually develop a liking for it. If you know the item is nutritionally beneficial, do not give up supplying it until you are really sure the pet does not like it.

Excess Feeding: Under normal conditions your pet will eat only sufficient food to meet its daily metabolic needs. These are directly related to its level of activity. However, if a pet is maintained for long periods in a small cage this is abnormal for such an active animal. It may develop syndromes, two of which are called polydipsia (excess drinking) and hyperphagia (excess eating).

These are involuntary compensatory actions to try and relieve boredom. Overeating may also be caused by animals that were underfed as babies, or which have been placed on slimming diets because they were becoming obese from being supplied high protein and fat diets. You can avoid these problems by ensuring your pet has ample exercise time out of its cage, and by supplying a balanced diet once the glider has settled into your home.

The Psychological Factor: There is a tendency with those concerned about nutritional content values to overlook the highly important

psychological factor involved with eating. It is of social importance to any gregarious species, such as sugar gliders. Hierarchy is established during feeding. Close friendships with others in the family unit are likewise established during this process.

Eating relaxes the nervous system, and the availability of a range of food items stimulates the appetite by the sight and smell of the foods on offer. Some food items take longer to eat than others. These facts all support the notion you should supply a range of items to maintain your pet's appetite and reduce the risk of psychological boredom. In so doing you will also limit the risk that certain

Not every sugar glider likes the same food. Try different fruits and vegetables, pieces of meat and dry cereals until you find a diet that satisfies your pet sugar glider.

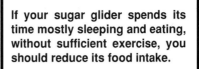

If your sugar glider spends its time mostly sleeping and eating, without sufficient exercise, you should reduce its food intake.

The great decision! Your sugar glider should get a daily offering of fresh and moist foods, semi-moist and dry foods as well. Feed very small portions.

ingredients may be missing from the diet.

SUGGESTED DIETARY FORMS

The diet of your pet should comprise a mixture of those foods which are fresh and moist, those which are semi-moist, and those which are dry. This will ensure the digestive system does not become biased towards dry or moist foods. It will mean you can feed small amounts of just about any item without the risk tummy upsets. The food can be given as salads, or as individual items.

SUGGESTED DIET FOODS

The items that can provide the animal protein part of your pet's diet are extensive. Most invertebrates obtained from your pet store, such as mealworms and crickets, are excellent. Some owners do not like to feed these livefoods to their pets, but they do provide needed beneficial nutrients, such as chitin, which will not be available in other foods. Do not feed invertebrates caught in your garden because they probably contain the eggs of parasites.

Other animal proteins can be given in the form of beef, its extracts, and other meats, cooked chicken and other poultry with the skin removed (it contains too much fat), canned and dry cat foods, scrambled, boiled or raw egg, cheese (low fat), lean hamburger, and slithers of boiled white fish.

The plant matter part of the diet covers most popular fruits, vegetables and seeds. Included in these would be apple, pear, grape,

plum, peach, strawberry, cherry, fig, date, pineapple, melon, orange, indeed, try any fruit you enjoy or could eat. Vegetables include peas, beans, carrots, boiled potatoes, celery, beet (including the leafy top), soybean, spinach, cauliflower, chive, tomato, turnip and cress. Some will have greater appeal than others. Fresh fruit and vegetables are better than canned because they do not contain the sweeteners and preservatives.

Seeds such as sunflower, panicum, safflower, niger, millet and other seeds commonly offered to cage birds can be supplied and provide good nutrients, as well as exercise for the pet's jaws and teeth. Most nuts will be enjoyed—if the shells prove too hard for your glider crack them open for them.

A small quantity of honey can be given as a treat, as can nectar of the sort supplied to softbilled birds (from your pet shop). But these should be supplied sparingly to avoid obesity.

Vitamin supplements, together with tonic foods, should be given with due caution. If the glider is eating a wide range of foods and is healthy it will have no need for these. Indeed, they could prove harmful in excess. If you suspect a dietary related deficiency in your pet discuss this with your vet who will suggest the appropriate supplement to supply while the diet is corrected.

QUANTITY AND TIMING OF MEALS

As a general guide, the amount to feed is that which will be consumed within about one hour with some left to be eaten later.

If all is eaten quickly, leaving little for later, you should increase the quantity at the next meal. If a lot is left you can reduce the quantity of the items not eaten. By this trial and error method you will arrive at the happy medium within a couple of days. Start with about one quarter of a cupful of assorted foods, plus dry cat food and meat— 2-3 mealworms per glider—or bits of meat.

It is important you always observe your pet while it eats, this being even more crucial when there are two or more sharing the housing. This is the only way you can be sure each pet is getting its share of each item. You will also become aware which are greedy feeders, which are slow dainty eaters. Be sure there are two or more feeding locations when a number of gliders live together.

Your pet's feeding habits can be a vital first sign of impending health problems. If the pet suddenly shows disinterest in its food, especially favored items, it will need very careful observation over the next 24 hours to see if normality returns, or if things are getting worse.

The main meal is best given in the early evening when these pets will start to become active. You could also give them a smaller meal in the morning. Always remove moist foods that are uneaten overnight. If two or more meals are given you must adjust the quantities so the daily rations are spread over these. Dry food can be left to be taken as wanted unless the pet starts to become obese, in which case they must be rationed.

Two meals per day are better than one because it spreads the digestive load more evenly, and discourages gluttony. In the wild gliders would steadily eat overnight. You should also try to ensure that meals are supplied at the same time—your pet will soon come to know when to expect its meal and will get quite excited to see what items are on that meal's menu.

To find out what your sugar glider likes the most, make a large offering and see which foods are eaten first.

Always try to make the meals interesting for your pet with a variety of items to tempt its palate. You could plan a weekly regimen in which all staple items are rotated, and in which special treats are given every so many days. Avoid the temptation to give your glider chocolates, cakes, and other stodgy high-calorie foods. These will increase the likelihood the pet will not eat all of its regular foods, and may become obese.

BREEDING Sugar Gliders

Sugar gliders are not especially difficult pets to breed. A consequence of this is there is no shortage of them. This helps keep prices at a reasonably modest level, but higher than in most other comparable exotic pets, such as hedgehogs, degus, duprasi and others. There is no benefit at all in pet owners allowing their pets to breed for their own sake—and especially so if they think they are going to make some quick easy money.

This is the root cause of many problems, not the least of which results in a rapid drop in prices. For this reason, unless you are extremely enthusiastic to breed quality sugar gliders on a regular basis, you should not allow your pets to breed. This means a male must not be housed with one or more females.

Sugar gliders are not very difficult to breed. Many people are now breeding them as a hobby.

Make sure that you are ready to breed your pets. Be sure you have enough space and a compatible breeding pair. What will you do with the babies? Do you want to keep them or sell them to your local pet shop?

The exotic mammal market is full of misinformation. Some of this is related to the investment value of breeding. You will no doubt hear of those who have made thousands of dollars breeding hedgehogs and sugar gliders. This is true but those days are already over. What you may not hear so often is how many people invested loaned money or savings into them too late—and lost it all!

They purchased too many breeding animals at a high price and before they could even breed salable age offspring the prices had fallen dramatically. Once pet owners start to breed their pets, the number of offspring, on a nationwide basis, multiplies at a rate far exceeding the level of demand at a given retail price. The owners have to reduce prices to sell. The downward spiral repeats itself very rapidly until the pet's retail price hits rock bottom.

BREEDING CONSIDERATIONS

Assuming you are satisfied these pets are not going to pay off your mortgage, the following are questions you should dwell on before getting underway.

1. Do you have the space and cash to purchase the needed extra accommodations in which to house the weaned offspring?

2. Do you have the extra time to devote to rearing and handling the youngsters in the period before they are sold?

3. Where will you sell the offspring? Your local pet shops will not be short of suppliers. You may have to advertise them, incurring extra time and cost, and you will not be short of competitors doing likewise. Never assume sales will be easy because they never are. This means your feeding costs, and maybe even vet bills, will go up. If you are thinking the market extends out of your state this will be a mistake. There are now sufficient gliders in those states where they are legal. Potential owners do not want to pay the extra cost of air freight: you will need documentation and vet health certificates. This means more time devoted to selling.

4. Have you the time to devote to a lot of unknowledgeable potential customers? If you advertise your offspring you will receive telephone calls from many potential buyers (often late in the evening) who will take up your time but never come to see the pets. Others will visit, taking up time, but will then purchase from someone else who is cheaper than you, or they will come purely as something to do with their spare time!

This is all part of the hard reality of being a breeder. Selling to pet stores overcomes most problems, but you must be prepared to sell the offspring at a lower price than retail.

GETTING STARTED

Your breeding stock purchase options have been discussed in an earlier chapter. It can be useful to obtain an unrelated pair, or even a

Walking around outside your home with a tame sugar glider in your pocket is NOT advised. The animal could easily escape and get lost.

If your sugar glider looks a bit under the weather, don't breed her. Only breed hand-tamed, very healthy animals.

trio of youngsters not yet at breeding age. This provides two breeding lines, both related via the initial male. Later, a second unrelated male can be purchased. You will then have a sound genetic pool for the future.

Purchasing youngsters also has the advantage that you will have gained practical experience maintaining these pets before they are old enough to breed. By that time you will have reflected on your enthusiasm for breeding: If you change your mind you can sell the single male, who will still be young.

BREEDING READINESS

Never allow your gliders to breed unless they are in the peak of condition. Certainly obese females,

in particular, should not be bred. This will risk birthing problems. Your breeders should be tame and accept a wide-ranging diet. This will have influence on the babies, who will copy their parents in their reactions to humans, and in their feeding habits.

When establishing an unrelated trio it is wise to introduce the females first so they are on friendly terms by the time the male is placed with them. When this happens the females will no doubt harass the male. Unless things get out of hand he will be able to cope and will slowly exert his dominance over them. The family unit is then established.

You are recommended to include two nestboxes in the cage so the

Before breeding, offer your sugar gliders some treats like fresh flower blossoms and other foods that they normally don't get in their daily regimen.

females can choose the one they like best. When females show no breeding willingness it may be because they do not like the position of the nestbox. It may not feel secure enough, is facing the wrong way, or is not high enough in the cage. Sometimes beginners assume a female (or the male) is not able to breed when the problem is actually environmental—this is a not uncommon happening in birds, especially those not well established in captivity.

It is wise to routinely deworm breeding stock to limit the potential for parasitic migration to the offspring via the placenta. Obtain the drugs from your veterinarian who will advise on the dosage. You should also ensure the stock has no external parasites, and the nestbox is totally free of these. If not they will multiply in the nestbox and create major problems at the least convenient time.

BREEDING - BASIC FACTS
The Female Estrus (Heat):
Sugar gliders are known as being polyestrus. This means they have a number of breeding periods during each year. The cycle (the time between the beginning of one estrus and ending with the beginning of the next) lasts for about 29 days. It is probable the female is most willing to accept mating a few days

into the cycle. In practical terms she will accept mating about once every month.

Sugar gliders can therefore be bred at any time during the year, especially under artificial light and heat conditions. As a general comment spring breedings are usually the best because of the longer days and warmer weather.

Gestation Period: This is the time between fertilization of the female's eggs to the birth of the babies. It is usually about 16 days, a very short period for an animal of this size. This is because the offspring of marsupials are born prematurely when compared to other placental mammals.

Litter Size: Normally one or two, rarely three.

Weaning Age: This is usually achieved when the babies are about 15 weeks old. They first leave the pouch when they are just over two months, having released their hold of a nipple about a month earlier. Once out of the pouch they start to sample solid foods. With each passing week they spend more time out of the pouch. They will cling to the mother's body, rather than climb into the marsupium, the older they get.

Litters Per Year: In the wild gliders normally have one litter per year—two if the first one dies for any reason. Under captive conditions they can theoretically have four. This would not be good for their general health and physical condition.

It would also adversely affect the vigor of their offspring.

Two litters would be the ideal. This allows the female to recuperate

Usually only one or two babies are produced per litter. The babies are weaned when they are about 15 weeks old. Certainly in 4 months they are old enough to be taken away from their mother.

her full condition. Any breeder whose object is to produce numbers rather than quality of offspring is a very poor breeder. They are invariably the sort who perpetuate faults in the population by applying no sound principles to their program.

FEEDING

When females are nursing babies they must be given extra food so the developing fetuses are never short of nutrients. At this time, and just prior to breeding, it is beneficial to supply a vitamin D_3 (cholecalciferol) supplement. This vitamin, which is also now considered to be a hormone, is important in helping (with others) to regulate the correct functioning of calcium.

Merely supplying extra calcium in powdered or other forms may not be beneficial if D_3 is not being generated in the liver. The entire chemical physiology controlling the absorption of calcium (and all other vitamins and minerals) is very complex. It has been noted that some sugar glider youngsters will develop paralysis of their hind legs, and some die from this condition. The cause has not yet been fully established. But it has been found that those supplied with vitamin D are much less prone to the problem. However, an excess of this vitamin may have deleterious effects, so it's important you always discuss the use of supplements with your vet.

It can also be added that both stress and high blood pressure may negatively alter the desired production of hormones needed to regulate calcium and other minerals. This is why the environment your pet lives in, its diet, and its temperament all influence the sugar glider's ability to produce healthy babies, and to nurse them to a healthy post-weaning state.

HUMAN IMPRINTING

Once the youngsters are leaving the pouch, and assuming the mother displays no concern or aggression, you should gradually start to gently handle them so they are imprinted on humans. This will make them far superior pets than those left unhandled within their family unit.

It's a well known fact that mammals and birds which are handreared make the most adorable of pets. However, handrearing is a long and risky process fraught with problems that may result in many babies dying. If you will devote as much time as possible interacting with the babies you will achieve the same state without the risks incumbent with taking a youngster from its mother.

DEVELOPING YOUR PROGRAM

As a serious breeder you will want to ensure your breeding program produces better and better gliders as it develops. The first step in this direction is you must maintain breeding records. These will detail all matings and their results. They will indicate the weights of babies as they grow, and which individuals, if any, have problems. You should maintain an individual record of all your retained stock.

Juveniles do not have the luxurious tails and fur growth of mature animals. If you intend breeding the sugar glider for profit, you should only breed the best animals you have and be sure to handle the babies as they mature.

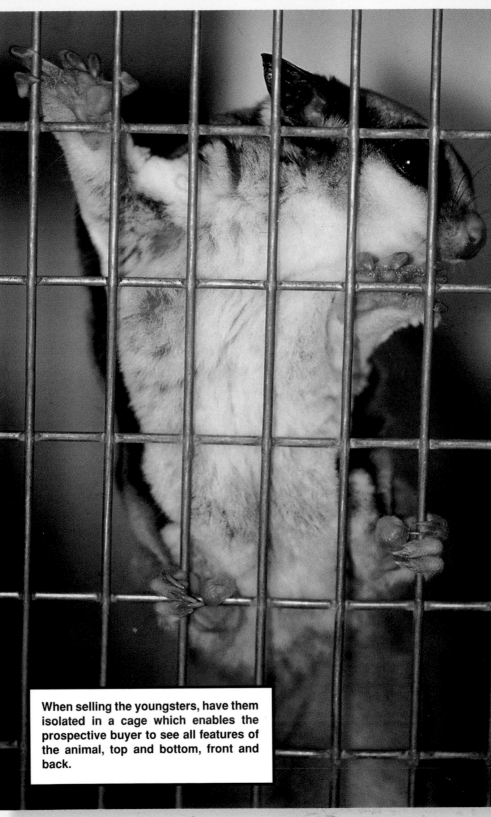

When selling the youngsters, have them isolated in a cage which enables the prospective buyer to see all features of the animal, top and bottom, front and back.

This will state the sire and dam of the individual, its birth date, any special markings it has, and to which partners it has been mated. There are many ways you can document your records. You are recommended to obtain *Sugar Gliders as Your New Pet,* another book on these animals published by TFH. This gives more detail on these matters than space permits here. It also discusses methods of selecting and grading your bred stock, an important need for the serious breeder.

SELLING THE YOUNGSTERS

When selling your surplus offspring you should try to provide the sort of service you would ideally want if you were a buyer. This means:

1. Never sell a youngster unless you are absolutely sure it is feeding independently of its mother.

2. Never sell a sugar glider unless you are satisfied it is in the peak of health.

3. Always provide the buyer,

and this includes pet shops, with a diet sheet so they know what the youngster has been fed. It helps if you also indicate what sort of floor and nestbox covering it is familiar with.

4. Contact the buyer after a few days to see if all is well. Be prepared to provide aftersales advice. The better this is, especially with pet shops, the more likely they are to want to purchase from you in the future. You will develop a sales market as you develop your breeding program.

For the serious breeder of sugar gliders there is a very interesting future. Color mutations will no doubt start to appear. These will offer tremendous potential, as they do in any animal hobby. But for the future opportunities to come your way you really must be dedicated to these pets, and willing to work very hard on your program, taking the ups and downs in your stride.

SUGAR GLIDERS AS YOUR NEW PET (TS-269) by Dennis Kelsey-Wood, was the first book ever written about sugar gliders and it is, even to this day, the best and most complete book on the subject.

The tail of a sugar glider, used for balancing and not for holding, is as long (or longer) than its body.

AVOIDING ILLNESS

L ike all other pets, the sugar glider is a hardy little animal not especially prone to any particular problems if well cared for. However, the caring process encompasses many areas of husbandry. If there is a breakdown in these, this dramatically increases the risk of illness. It is not possible to remove the potential for a pet to become ill. Your objective is to minimize the likelihood of things going wrong by paying attention to those aspects that will create problems if they are neglected. Rather than dealing with illness it is far better to try and avoid it in the first place. This chapter is written with this in mind, rather than cataloging potential diseases, conditions and their treatments, which is of no benefit to you in practical terms.

You should be constantly observing your pet sugar glider for any abnormality. Even their claws must be trimmed from time to time.

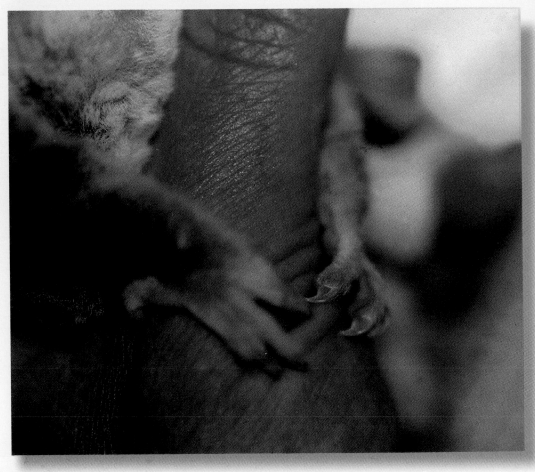

Sugar gliders pick up pathogens like humans, via the air, their food or the failure of their immune systems to protect them from the usual diseases awaiting their chance to infect. Protect your sugar glider as best you can.

THE SOURCES OF PROBLEMS

Pathogens (disease-causing organisms) are ever present in the air, on foods, on and in your pets, on you—indeed they are everywhere. The vast majority present no problems if they are not allowed to proliferate to the degree your glider's immune system is overwhelmed. When this happens, that's when things start to go wrong.

The immune system comprises elements and compounds in the body, as well as organisms in their many forms, that work to eradicate, or limit, any foreign bodies that are attempting to interrupt the efficiency of body metabolism. The system must be created, maintained, and protected from being overwhelmed.

It is created and maintained by the diet of the pet. It is protected by your having control over the immediate area in which your pet lives. If you think of health care in these terms you should have no problems in maintaining good health in your pets.

The major sources of husbandry errors are:

1. The diet is inadequate to meet the needs of normal body metabolism. It may be lacking in certain proteins, carbohydrates, vitamins, minerals, or water.

2. The immediate and proximinal environment is conducive to the rapid multiplication of pathogens. This is invariably on a continual and increasingly negative basis. In other words the pet's housing is dirty, and so is the immediate area around this.

Alternatively, or concurrently with this situation, the temperature is too high, too low, or is fluctuating beyond healthy limitations.

3. The environment of the pet is stressful to the degree it is suppressing the normal functioning of the immune system. It may be encouraging abnormal behavior patterns that of themselves are likely to create health problems.

Once any or all of these situations is applicable, and the pet becomes ill, many owners compound the problem in the following ways:

1. They fail to take appropriate measures having established things are not as they should be.

2. They seek 'cheap' diagnosis and treatment suggestions and will accept this from people not qualified to give it. This includes other pet owners, breeders, and pet shop assistants. Some of these may indeed have an excellent knowledge of health subjects, but you cannot be sure of this if they have no qualifications. Their knowledge in certain areas of management may be the best you can get from any source, but this should not be assumed where health matters are concerned.

Indeed, those with such knowledge will be the very ones who will tell you exactly what this author is telling you. The only person you should listen to with respect to diagnosis and treatments is your vet—and even he will be the first to admit he doesn't know everything.

Let us review crucial areas of husbandry that you can, and should, understand and apply. It will limit your need to visit the vet.

If a newly acquired sugar glider falls ill, it might be because you have not provided a stress-free environment. Ask the advice of an experienced veterinarian.

If you have to feed medicine to your pet, it is easiest given by hand via a morsel laced with the medicine. That's one advantage of having a very tame pet.

NUTRITION

The health of your pet is wholly determined first and foremost by the foods it eats. This provides the body with the capacity to develop its immune system to the maximum of its potential. Never skimp costs. Be sure all foods are fresh and stored where they will remain in that state—in the refrigerator, or in a cool, airy, dark cupboard.

There is a tendency these days for pet owners to rely heavily on commercially prepared foods. These are convenient, and they do help to ensure important vitamins and minerals are provided. However, their labels and advertising often make claims that bend reality. Never rely on the total accuracy of such claims, nor let convenience dictate what you feed. You cannot better a regimen that is based on supplying a varied diet. It minimizes the risk of important nutrients missing, and it does reduce stress levels.

HYGIENE

This is a much abused area of husbandry. It is so easy to put off until tomorrow that which should be done today. We are all guilty of it, and it gives pathogens the extra time to proliferate. Major potential weaknesses in general husbandry are:

1. Cage bars not being cleaned regularly. Your glider will rub its snout on the bars and this is one often overlooked way in which pathogens can gain access to its mouth, nose, and eyes.

2. Cracked or worn food/water vessels not replaced. Bacteria can survive quite high temperatures in food receptacle cracks, are not always removed by regular washing of the vessels. They can then spread to the food, thence into the gliders digestive and respiratory tracts. Replace food dishes the moment you see cracks or the surfaces are worn—as with those made of plastic.

3. Total cleaning of the cage not thorough. Hurried cleaning usually results in dirt and fecal matter remaining in crevices or corners. These become a constant potential source of pathogenic colonization. Also, merely covering up dirty floor covering with fresh material may give the illusion of cleanliness, but it will increase the rate of bacterial action on that below it. If the cage looks messy, clean it.

Perches and branches should be cleaned daily and replaced when worn. They are places on which your glider will defecate and rub its snout.

4. Hands not routinely washed. Always wash your hands before and after handling your pet. This is very important if you have been gardening because soil is a vast reservoir of dangerous organisms just waiting for someone to transport them into the area of a potential host. Children are excellent transporters!

Remember also, if you have been visiting friends with an ill pet, or visiting animal shows, pet shops, or any other place where there is a large pet population you could easily transport pathogens into your home. Breeders in particular should always wear nylon over clothes when attending routine chores.

STRESS

This is a very important precursor of problems. Possibly its biggest source is lack of space. This denies your pet the potential to exercise and explore. Stressors that deny or limit a natural wild action are always the ones most likely to have an effect on the individual.

On this basis, others will be harassment by a bully in a family unit such that the pet cannot escape this. Excessive handling, and interruption when the pet is sleeping are two examples. Children are likely to be the problem here.

Noises the pet finds uncomfortable are another stress. These can be difficult to pinpoint, so it is a case of considering which might frighten or annoy you if you did not know what they were— vacuum cleaners, power tools and their like which suddenly start and stop.

A dog or a cat that persists in trying to get at the glider while in its cage will also be a stressor. Excessive heat, cold and humidity are known stressors, as is a deficiency in the diet.

Some pets are affected by stress more than others, this being influenced by their breeding, and the way they were reared as babies.

The effects of stress are numerous. Firstly, stress suppresses normal functioning of the immune system, making the pet more vulnerable to illness. It can result in aggression, or undue timidity and nervousness. It is the root cause of many abnormal behavior patterns. These include stereotyped pacing and climbing, self-mutilation (excessive biting

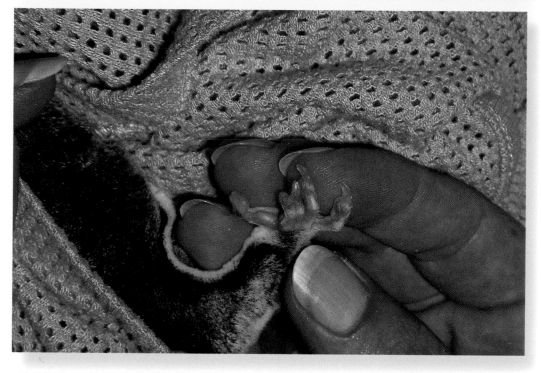

Above: Wrap your sugar glider in a soft, woven bag preparatory to clipping its claws. *Below:* Use a typical nail clipper but be sure you only clip off the very tip of the nail. Don't cut the quick.

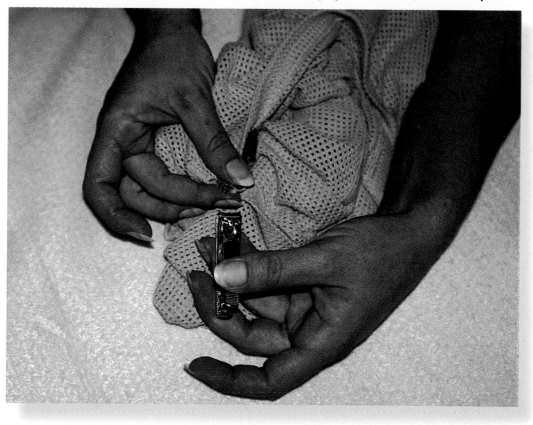

and scratching to the point wounds are created), eating of foreign matter, such as feces, wood, fur, floor covering, and excessive preening of another family member to the point hair is denuded.

It may induce overeating or drinking, and can be the cause of failure to breed, abandonment of offspring, or cannibalism on them. It may result in the female not being able to nurse the babies correctly. When gliders are in a pair or family unit stress will be less of a problem than with a single pet. This is because they are by nature very social animals. Lack of space will be the prime cause of problems for family units.

In a number of instances the problems discussed may have alternative causes, making stress a difficult problem to identify. If any of the problems discussed are displayed in your pet you should correct the situation as soon as possible.

Usually, once a stressor is removed, the problem it created will cease, but not always. This is especially so with changes in behavior, which can become habits difficult to break. For example, pacing and self mutilation due to boredom. In these instances it may help if the cage is moved to a new location.

It may also be that any replacement housing, though larger, is still too small or that the pet, if the only glider, lacks out of cage time and/or interacting with its owner.

Is The Pet Ill?

To determine whether a pet is ill is normally not difficult to assess. It will be based on one or both of two situations.

Behavior: Any changes in the normal behavior pattern of a glider should be viewed with concern. Only by knowing the habits of your pet can you decide what is normal, but generally the following are abnormal conditions.

Sudden loss of appetite, or excess eating. Reduction in drinking without any change in the diet having taken place (an increase in moist foods would reduce the water taken by drinking, and the reverse). The cause is internal and will need veterinary advice.

Listlessness and general lethargy. Gliders are active animals and a sudden reduction in activity will have some cause, usually an internal problem. Excessive scratching will be a sign of stress, parasites, or an internal problem.

Difficulty in passing urine or fecal matter. This is a gastro-intestinal problem and the vet's advice should be sought. Unusual noises from the pet when it's in a lethargic state. These are probably cries of pain. Consult the vet immediately.

Reluctance to being handled. This is either due to an injury not obviously apparent, or an internal problem causing pain.

Retreating to a darkened location. The pet possibly has an eye problem so is avoiding bright light. In both instances consult your vet.

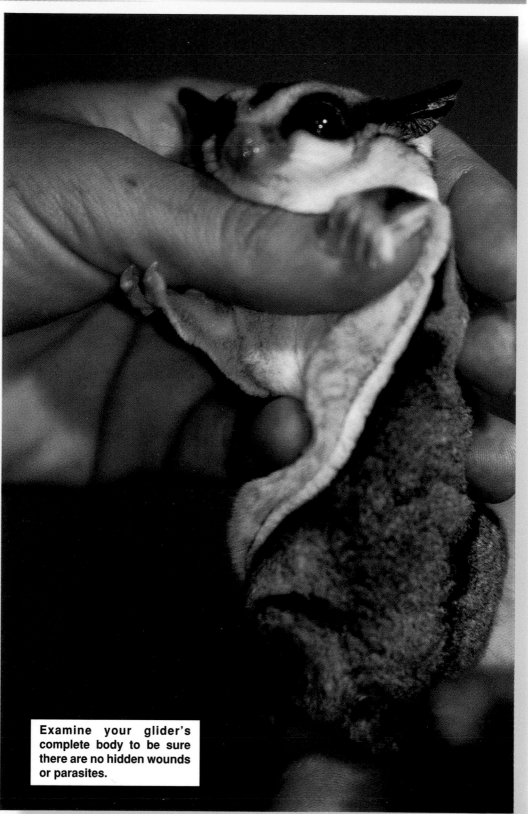

Examine your glider's complete body to be sure there are no hidden wounds or parasites.

Examine your sugar glider's face carefully. Weeping eyes are a sure sign of a physical problem.

Physical Signs: Any signs, such as weeping eyes, loss of fur, lumps and abrasions, can only be manifest if something is wrong. The problem may be of external or internal origin—or both.

Diarrhea is an obvious physical indicator of a problem, minor or major. If the fecal matter or urine is blood-streaked consult the vet

display signs of a chill because the temperature dropped for a while after a power outage, or because it was windy when its cage was placed outdoors for a while. Its fecal matter may be more liquid than normal because it ate more than usual of a certain food, or one it is not familiar with.

It may have been more active

If your pet sugar glider refuses to come out of his nest, even at night or to feed, then you know something serious is wrong.

immediately. The greater the number of physical signs displayed the more advanced the problem is, and the greater the urgency for seeking professional diagnosis and treatment.

WHEN TO REACT TO ILLNESS

Your sugar glider, like we humans, can have its good and bad days. Sometimes it may

than usual and is tired when it would normally be running around. These are all temporary conditions that will return to normal within 12-24 hours. If a behavior change, or a physical sign, persists beyond this time the vet should be consulted. But if the signs are obviously more worrying do not delay in contacting your vet.

How To React

Once you are satisfied your pet is ill you should note when you first suspected the problem, and how quickly the situation has deteriorated. Have other signs been added to the first ones?

Has there been any sort of your pets been ill recently, and is there any chance the pet may have gained access to a chemical that could be toxic? Now contact your vet.

If you cannot immediately do this, or visit the clinic, isolate the pet from other pets or gliders. Be

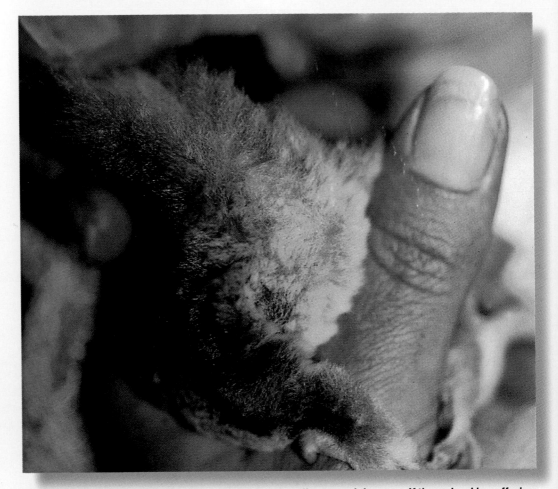

Check the anus of your sugar glider to look for cleanliness and dryness. If the animal is suffering from diarrhea or worms, its anus might be the first place you'll notice them.

change in the pet's food or environment that could be related to the problem? You may have been somewhere where a pet was ill, or food item may have been 'off' when you fed it. If livefoods were fed what was the source? Have any other of sure the location is warm, the lighting subdued. Clean the housing very thoroughly. If diarrhea is present withhold moist foods for 12 hours pending the advice of your vet, but maintain the water supply.

Once you are convinced your pet sugar glider is sick, don't wait until it gets sicker. Contact someone who knows more than you, either a breeder, a pet shop who sells sugar gliders or a veterinarian who knows small animals.

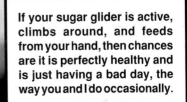

If your sugar glider is active, climbs around, and feeds from your hand, then chances are it is perfectly healthy and is just having a bad day, the way you and I do occasionally.

DIAGNOSIS

Although many pet owners think an illness can be diagnosed via the telephone, based on observed signs, this is rarely the case. Invariably your vet needs to see the pet, and can either make a pragmatic diagnosis, or will need to conduct various tests from fecal matter, skin scrapings, or blood

TREATMENTS

Modern medicines can be used in three ways. Topical, meaning they are applied to the surface of the skin, orally, meaning they are swallowed by the pet, or injections given under the skin, or directly into muscles or blood vessels. The seriousness of the illness, its advancement state, its cause, and

Understand that an abrupt change in your pet's behavior, from a friendly animal to a shy one, almost always means a problem. Consult your veterinarian quickly.

samples. Unless the causal organism, or group of these, can be specifically identified any treatment would be based on an element of gamble.

You must appreciate that many physically abnormal signs are common to a multitude of potential causes, which is why the vet must see the pet and proceed from that point.

the temperament of the pet will influence which of these is best where there is a choice.

A treatment may have a broad spectrum of application, or it may be species or group specific. If the cause cannot be positively identified a broad spectrum antibiotic will invariably be used. If the species can be identified it is superior to use a species-specific drug on it.

Some drugs have a low risk of negative side effects, others a higher risk. Some will not be dangerous if slightly in excess, others could be fatal if given beyond a certain dosage. Some are safe if used in isolation of other drugs, others are dangerous because they may interact, or double up on a common compound, if used together.

stored within given temperature ranges. Never gamble your pet's life to try and save a few dollars.

PARASITES

By far the majority of diseases and negative conditions in your pet are the result of parasites. These consume the tissue or organs of their host. In so doing they create lesions that allow secondary

If your Sugar glider becomes ill, only use drugs recommended or prescribed by a veterinarian familiar with small animals.

These facts are given to you so you can appreciate that any advice other than that of a vet could be fatal to your pet. It should also be added that all medicines have a very definite shelf or exposure life after which they can be dangerous or ineffective. They must also be

conditions (other parasites) to take up residence, making the situation more dangerous. Some parasites, apart from the direct damage they do, act as vectors (carriers) for other parasites that are within them, but not creating undue problems for the vector.

If you are concerned about your pet sugar glider, and you have more than one, isolate the sick animal in a small cage so you can observe it better and, if the situation so requires, you can cover up the cage and take the animal, cage and all, to visit the vet.

Fleas, mites, lice and worms are common examples. Other vectors are flies, birds, and other animals and pets. These may not directly cause diseases in your glider (they do not parasitize it) but cause them by depositing eggs, larvae, or adults of parasites onto the pet, onto its food or its housing.

Some parasites seen on your pet, such as fleas, may not actually be parasitic on them—they may be species-specific to other animals or pets. They have alighted on the glider by accident. They will move on, or die, not having reproduced on your glider. But you will not know this. Those seen in numbers are probably parasitic. Their fecal matter will be in the form of clusters of tiny dark specks.

Mite activity will be seen in the form of a white powder at the base of hairs. The mites burrow into the hairs destroying them and their follicles. The hair usually becomes dry and lifeless.

Fleas and mites are visible to the naked eye, especially if a hand lens is used. Regular examination of your pet is a must so they are spotted as soon as possible and not able to proliferate.

Control of external parasites is not a problem with modern drugs from your vet. Internal parasites, such as tape– and roundworms, can be identified via fecal samples. Egg counts establish the level of infestation. The treatment mentioned is effective on these, though other worm species (heart and lung) may require other drugs.

When treating for any parasites it is essential the housing and its immediate area are also treated. Repeat treatments are usually obligatory some days later to eradicate adults or larvae hatched from eggs not killed at the first treatment.

Finally, once an illness has been overcome make every effort to rectify the causal problem if it's husbandry based. If not, it will likely happen again. In the event a glider dies without displaying any physical or behavioral signs, an autopsy by your vet would be prudent. For a breeder, it should be regarded as essential to try and establish the cause—it might save others going the same way.

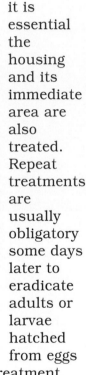

Fleas, mites and ticks are easily controllable. Don't let perpetual scratching ruin an otherwise perfect pet.

SUGAR GLIDER PRIMER

Scientific Name: *Petaurus breviceps*
Order: Marsupialia
Family: Petauridea
Distribution: Australia, Indonesia
Some Pacific islands
Length: Head & Tail 24-31cm (9-12in)
Weight: Circa 135g (4.8oz)
Number Digits: 5 on each foot
Longevity: Average 8-10, maximum 14 years
Social Status: Pairs or family groups in the wild
Required Temp/Humidity: 70-80°F (21-27°C.
R.H. 50-65%
Breeding Age: Females about 8 months,
males older
Estrus Cycle: Polyestrus, 29 days average
Gestation Period: Average 16 days
Litter Size: 1-2, rarely 3
Leave Pouch: About 70 days of age
Weaning: 105 days (15 weeks) average
Feeding Type: Omnivorous (fruits, vegetables,
  plants, grain, invertebrates and meat)
Housing: Large cage or indoor aviary—as much
  height as possible, climbing perches or branches
  plus nestbox essential

INDEX

Page numbers in **boldface** refer to illustrations.